SHARKS

GET UP CLOSE TO NATURE'S FIERCEST PREDATORS

BEN HUBBARD

THE FRILLED SHARK
SWIMS IN DEEP WATERS
AND IS RARELY SEEN AT
THE SURFACE.

THIS IS A CARLTON BOOK

Text, design, and illustration © Carlton Books Limited 2019
Published in 2019 by Carlton Books Limited
An imprint of the Carlton Publishing Group
20 Mortimer Street, London W1T 3JW.

A catalogue record for this book is available from the British
Library.

ISBN: 978-1-78312-451-0

Printed in Dubai

Editors: Alexandra Koken
Design: Punch Bowl Design
Art Editor: Dani Lurie
CGI Artwork: Ryan Forshaw
Picture Research: Steve Behan

THE ELEPHANT SHARK
IS ONE OF THE
OCEAN'S STRANGER
CREATURES.

CONTENTS

A GREAT WHITE'S SERRATED TEETH ARE DESIGNED FOR SLICING OFF CHUNKS OF FLESH.

ELECTRONIC TAGS LIKE THIS ONE ALLOW SCIENTISTS TO TRACK SHARK MOVEMENTS.

Below the surface of the sea is a mysterious world, largely unexplored by humans. It is a world ruled by ancient, fearsome creatures. They have existed for over 400 million years and dominated the ocean long before dinosaurs roamed the earth. Today, these predators hunt all marine habitats and their name alone can strike terror into human hearts: sharks.

Sharks are perfectly built hunters that have changed little over their millions of years of evolution. The most powerful sharks can outrun a speed boat, bite through a turtle shell and smell blood from hundreds of metres away. But not all members of the shark family are bloodthirsty killers. Some sharks are longer than a bus and weigh more than three elephants, but are no threat to humans. Other sharks are so small they could fit into the palm of your hand.

People have always been fascinated by sharks. Shark stories feature in legends, books, films and documentaries. A shark attack is always headline news – a terrifying reminder that sharks, and not humans, are the top predators of the ocean.

I have been crazy about sharks since childhood. From the shark stories I read as a boy, to my first brush with a great white as a teenager, sharks have always been a huge part of my life. Over the years as I observed, tagged and studied sharks around the world my fear turned into respect as I began to understand and admire these animals. As we delve deep into the watery world of sharks over the following pages, I hope that you will learn to better understand this magnificent and often misunderstood creature too.

Ben Hubbard
Shark Biologist

Sharks hunt in every sea and ocean on Earth: from the dark, inky depths where light cannot enter, to the warm, transparent shallows where people paddle. Whenever you set foot into the water, you are entering shark territory.

Sharks are often shown as the sleek, torpedo-shaped terror of the seas, armed with a powerful tail, six deadly senses and several rows of sharp, serrated teeth. But there are 510 known species of shark – they come in a vast variety of different shapes and sizes.

AMAZING ADAPTATIONS

When I began working as a shark biologist I was amazed by the different sharks I saw. The spotted wobbegong, for example, is flat and camouflaged, and lies on the seabed like a carpet waiting to ambush its prey. Epaulette sharks are reef dwellers that can walk back to the sea on their pectoral fins when the tide goes out and leaves them stranded on dry land. But no sharks grabbed my attention like the "man eaters". The great white, the bull shark and the tiger shark stand out among the 30 or so species known to attack humans. Nicknamed the "big three", they are the most dangerous sharks on Earth.

THIS BANDED WOBBEGONG SHARK IS A PERFECTLY ADAPTED AMBUSH PREDATOR THAT LIES IN WAIT ON THE OCEAN FLOOR.

THIS EPAULETTE
SHARK'S YELLOW AND
BROWN COLOURING
PROVIDES EFFECTIVE
CAMOUFLAGE.

SHARK DESIGN

All sharks are Chondrichthyes. Members of
this fish family have skeletons made of tough,
rubbery tissue called cartilage, instead of
bone. Sharks have several other key features
in common: they all breathe through five to
seven gills on their sides; have skin made up
of thousands of tiny enamel teeth; and have
multiple rows of teeth. Sharks are natural
predators, born to hunt, kill and devour other
creatures to survive.

MOST SHARKS, SUCH AS
THIS BASKING SHARK, HAVE
FIVE GILLS ON EACH SIDE OF
THEIR HEADS.

As a boy I spent hours
gazing at this painting.
It shows the shark attack
of 14-year-old cabin boy
Brook Watson in Havana
harbour, Cuba, in 1749. The
tiger shark bit Brook's foot
clean off and it took three
attempts to rescue him.
Brook had to have his leg
amputated, but he later
became Lord Mayor
of London.

As a young boy I made an amazing discovery along the coastal cliffs where we lived. There, embedded in the rock, was a huge fossil of an ancient shark tooth. The tooth was so large that I needed two hands to carry it. It was the remains of a massive shark called a megalodon.

MONSTER MEGALODON

The mighty megalodon roamed the seas from two to 20 million years ago, and is the largest shark that ever lived. Known as Carcharodon megladon, or "big tooth", Megalodon was a super predator that could grow up to 18 metres long and weighed over 50 tonnes. Megalodon was the size of a blue whale and looked like a great white, but it would have made a morsel of any modern shark. With jaws over 2 metres wide, Megalodon had the most powerful bite in history. The shark could snap its jaws shut with over 18 tonnes of force — that's three times more powerful than the 6-tonne bite of a T-rex! Human beings, by comparison, only bite with a feeble 80 kilograms of force.

A GREAT WHITE TOOTH IS SHOWN ALONGSIDE THE FOSSIL OF THE PREHISTORIC MEGALODON, THE LARGEST SHARK THAT EVER LIVED.

THE FIRST SHARKS

One of the earliest sharks, called Cladoselache, lived around 380 million years ago but closely resembled today's frilled shark. Like Cladoselache, the frilled shark has a mouth at the end rather than the underside of its head – similar to many modern sharks. Many Cladoselache fossils have been found in North America. Ancient shark skeletons, teeth and skin became fossilized when the dead fish fell to the bottom of the sea and were covered with sand and sediment. The body parts rotted away over time, leaving a perfect imprint – or fossil – behind.

TRIDENT-SHAPED TEETH ARE TYPICAL OF SHARKS SUCH AS THE FRILLED SHARK.

1.7 METRES |·····| HUMAN

5.5 METRES |················| GREAT WHITE SHARK

12 METRES |··························| MEGALODON (MINIMUM)

18 METRES |································| MEGALODON (MAXIMUM)

DANGER LURKS

Sharks soundlessly patrol almost all large bodies of water, from the warm waters of the tropics to the freezing seas of the polar regions. There are sharks in every marine habitat: from mangroves, rocky shores and coral reefs, to estuaries and the open ocean. Pelagic sharks prefer the open ocean, and include the three largest sharks: the whale shark, the basking shark and the megamouth shark as well as top predators, such as the great white and the oceanic whitetip. These powerful hunters can travel for thousands of miles to mate and find prey. Other sharks have adapted to survive in fresh water. The aggressive bull shark has been known to leave its sea reef habitat and swim for 4,000 kilometres up rivers such as the Amazon and Mississippi to find food.

THIS ZEBRA HORN SHARK SPENDS MOST OF ITS TIME RESTING ON THE OCEAN FLOOR, LYING IN WAIT.

REMORAS ARE SMALL FISH THAT SWIM WITH LARGE SHARKS AND FEED OFF THEIR SCRAPS.

THE EXTRAORDINARY
GREENLAND SHARK
LIVES IN DARKNESS
AND HUNTS BY ITS
SENSE OF SMELL.

DEEP DWELLERS

Benthic sharks dwell on the ocean floor, and include the wobbegong, angelshark and zebra horn shark. These small sharks are typically ambush hunters that stay hidden while they lie in wait for their prey. They are equipped with incredible eyesight and lightning-fast reflexes. A larger relative lives in the freezing, black waters under the Arctic ice. The Greenland shark relies on its phenomenal sense of smell to find food such as rotting carcasses that have drifted under the ice. Most Greenland sharks have a parasite that attaches and feeds on the outside of its eyeball, which slowly makes the shark blind.

Global warming and overfishing is causing some sharks to change their behaviour and move to different areas to find food. Often, this brings them closer to people, and swimmers, surfers, paddlers and kayakers soon become targets.

Sharks are everywhere, but most favour particular habitats. This world map shows where some of the best-known sharks are commonly found.

16

MAP LEGEND

- Great white shark
- Megamouth shark
- Tiger shark
- Frilled shark
- Scalloped hammerhead shark

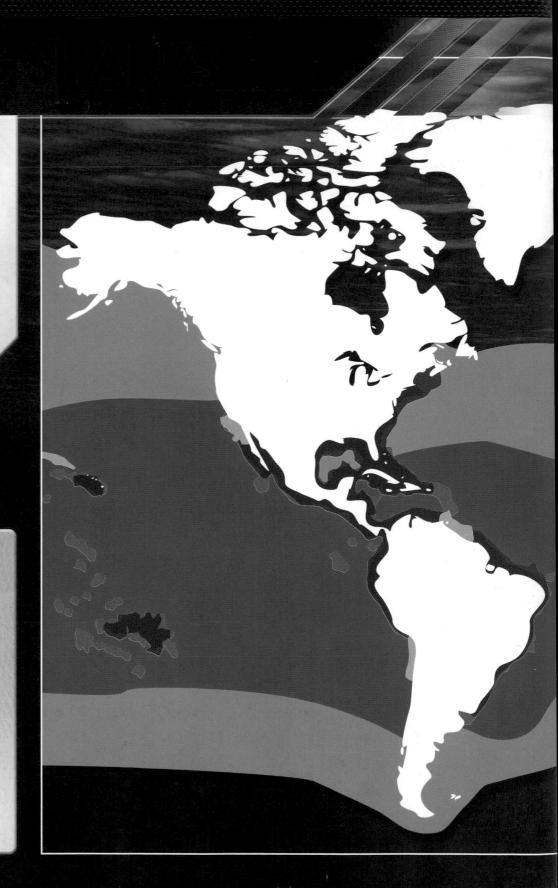

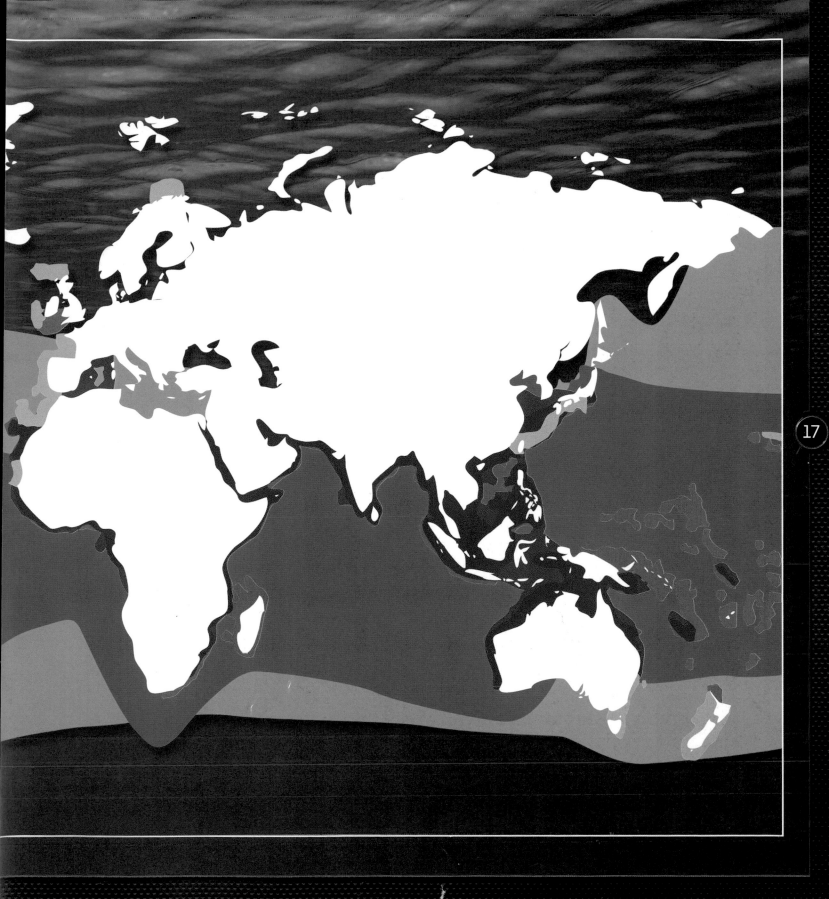

For many, the great white shark is the stuff of nightmares. It is the largest predatory fish on Earth: a supreme, solitary hunter that combines the skills of stealth, strength and speed to kill and consume large mammals. Over a third of shark attacks on humans are inflicted by great whites. I was the victim of one such attack.

SHOCKING SURPRISE

From underneath, the great white's underside looks like the bright surface of the water; from above, its grey back blends in with the rocks below. Concealed by its colouring, the great white has perfected the surprise attack. After sinking its huge jaws into its prey, the shark shakes its head violently from side to side to saw off chunks of flesh. Seabirds, turtles and rays to sea lions, seals, dolphins and even small whales are all on the menu.

The great white can cruise for vast distances in search of prey. I once tracked a great white that travelled from Africa to Australia and back again in nine months, a journey of close to 20,000 kilometres. Great whites are comfortable in all water temperatures because they are warm-blooded. This also makes the great white a more efficient killer: with warmed-up muscles, it can very quickly accelerate to catch its prey.

ALSO KNOWN AS THE WHITE POINTER, BLUE POINTER, WHITE SHARK, AND WHITE DEATH, FEW PREDATORS RIVAL THE FEROCIOUS GREAT WHITE.

SHARKS STATS

NAME: Great white shark (*Carcharodon carcharias*)

LENGTH: 1.8–6.4 metres

WEIGHT: Up to two tonnes

COLOUR: Grey, brown and bluish with a white underside

RANGE: Worldwide from the shallows to depths of 1,200 metres

LIFE SPAN: 40+ years

My speciality is finding and tagging sharks that have attacked people, such as a great white that terrorized the coastline of Western Australia. It did not take me long to find and tag this five-metre-long rogue shark with a special transmitter. The transmitter then sent an alert via Twitter to coastguards when the shark came close to shore. After a few weeks, the shark departed Western Australia to find easier prey elsewhere.

GREAT WHITES ARE OFTEN KNOWN TO BREACH THE WATER WHILE TAKING THEIR PREY FROM THE SURFACE.

To: Ben Hubbard

From: The Shark Biological Society

Subject: Shark tracking assignment

Dear Mr Hubbard,

We suspect the recent shark attacks in Western Australia may be the work of a lone shark. Please travel to Australia to locate, tag and track this shark. Your plane tickets are in the post. Good luck and keep us up to date with developments.

Yours sincerely,
Aggie Rogozinska
The Shark Biological Society

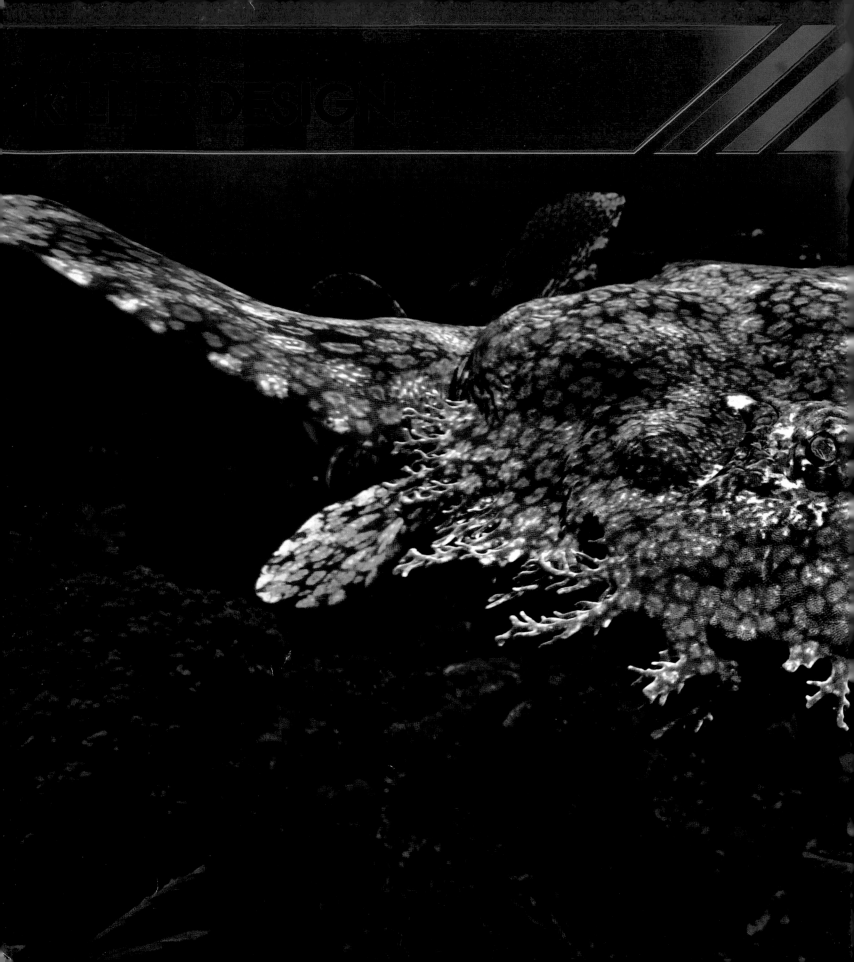

Sharks are such successful predators that their basic body design has barely changed in over 350 million years. Each shark is born with a mouth full of teeth, a powerful tail for swimming and super senses. But while all sharks share these characteristics, some have adapted in strange and unexpected ways.

Sharks are far more than killing machines. They are complex creatures with bodies well adapted to the harsh and difficult ocean environment. Every part of a shark's body plays a vital role in its struggle for survival, from its guts to its gills.

INSIDES

With oxygen-rich blood circulating around its body, a shark can grow, repair injuries and hunt. One of a shark's most important organs is its oil-rich liver, which provides energy during hungry periods and helps keep the creature buoyant in the water.

SKIN

Overlapping rows of tiny denticles make up a shark's skin and create a perfectly smooth surface for gliding through water. Shark skin colours vary according to the creature's habitat, from the grey, blue and white stripes of the tiger shark, to the yellow, green and brown camouflage of the spotted wobbegong.

GILLS

Sharks breathe through gills located on either side of their bodies. As water passes into a shark's mouth, the gills absorb oxygen through the open gill slits. Sharks need a constant supply of new water to survive, which most achieve by swimming forwards.

FINS

A shark uses its fins to control its movements in the water. It adjusts the angles of its pectoral fins to go up, down, left, right or vary its speed. The shark's dorsal fins – which can often be seen when it swims near the surface – stop it from rolling in the water, as does its anal fin.

TAIL

A shark beats its tail from side to side to propel itself through the water. The tail has two sections: a top lobe and a bottom lobe. The top lobe is often larger than the bottom, which produces lift in the water and helps stop the shark from sinking while it swims.

A shark's sleek physique and deadly senses make them the most feared fish in the world. We have reason to be scared: there is no contest between a shark and human in the water. However, a swimmer only has a one in 11.5 million chance of being bitten by a shark.

DANGER

KILLER BITE

Teeth are a shark's ultimate weapons. They are used for attack, defence and to tear chunks of flesh from their victims. Many sharks have protruding jaws. The great white pushes out its jaws to spear a victim on its long, narrow teeth. Shortfin makos have a lower jaw full of thin, slightly curved teeth, which are perfect for catching and holding slippery fish. The Port Jackson shark has sharp front teeth and flat back teeth for grinding up crabs, clams and other shelled creatures. However, the largest sharks of all – the megamouth, basking and whale sharks – have tiny teeth that are not even used for eating. Instead, they swallow huge mouthfuls of water and filter out plankton, krill and shrimp, through comb-like rakes on their gills.

ANATOMY OF A TOOTH

A shark's teeth are bigger versions of the thousands of denticles that make up its skin. Each tooth is made from a hard substance called dentine and covered in tough enamel. A shark is constantly growing new teeth, from the moment it begins developing as an embryo until the time of its death. When teeth are lost or wear out, new ones comes up to replace them. A shark can get through as many as 20,000 teeth in its lifetime.

A WHALE SHARK REVEALS ITS MASSIVE GAPE AS IT FEEDS ON PLANKTON.

To: The Shark Biological Society

From: Ben Hubbard

Dear Aggie,

Please find images of my new method for investigating the species of shark responsible for the recent attacks in California. By using the jaws of a great white to bite into a clay block, I was able to compare the imprint with the teeth-marks left in the leg of one of the surfers. This means I can confirm the attacks were carried out by a great white and not a mako, as previously thought.

Yours sincerely,
Ben Hubbard

CONVEYOR-BELT ROWS OF TEETH ARE AMONG THE REASONS FOR ITS EVOLUTIONARY SUCCESS.

THIS GREAT WHITE SHARK'S TEETH GIVE IT A FEARSOME APPEARANCE.

Like humans, sharks have the five senses of touch, taste, smell, sight and hearing. But they also have a spectacular sixth sense, which allows them to pick up electrical signals in the water. This helps them detect the movement of their prey, avoid predators and navigate the world's oceans.

HEARING

Sharks have inner ears which are only visible through two small holes behind their eyes. Although small, shark ears can pick up a low-frequency sound from several kilometres away and tell which direction it is coming from.

SIGHT

Most sharks have excellent vision. Some sharks have large eyes to see in dark water while others have special cells that filter bright sunlight. Many sharks have a protective membrane that covers their eyeballs while they attack. A great white simply rolls its eyes back into its head as it lunges towards its prey.

TOUCH

Sharks detect touch through nerves underneath their skin. Some species, such as the nurse shark, also have special barbels on their snouts to feel for prey buried in the seabed. Sharks can also pick up distant vibrations in the water with a "lateral line" – a row of small pores on each side of their body.

SIXTH SENSE

Tiny "electroreceptor" organs on a shark's snout allows it to pick up the electrical signals that all living creatures produce. This sixth sense also detects manmade objects, such as boats and metal cages. Many scientists believe sharks use this sixth sense to navigate long distances across the Earth's oceans.

SMELL

Sharks can detect fish fluids and blood in the water from hundreds of metres away. A shark's nostrils are located at the end of its snout and by swinging its head from side to side it can pick up the direction a smell is coming from.

TASTE

The tastebuds of most sharks are located on bumps in their mouths, so unluckily for humans they usually taste by taking a bite. Most sharks leave humans alone after taking a first bite to see whether we are food. Others, such as tiger sharks, have been known to keep on eating.

While investigating the waters around Barbados, I noticed several oceanic whitetip sharks tailing my boat. After tagging and tracking some of the sharks, I found that they drew near whenever the engine slowed down. The sharks had learned that the sound of the boat stopping meant a fish had been caught – their chance to steal the catch!

All nine species of hammerhead sharks are simple to identify because of their distinctive hammer-shaped heads. Attacks involving hammerheads are rare, so I was surprised when several kayakers reported being attacked by hammerheads in the waters of Cocos Island, Costa Rica. And when I arrived, I found not one or two hammerheads — but dozens.

28

SHARK SCHOOL

On Cocos Island I compared the bite marks on the kayaks against an imprint of a scalloped hammerhead's jaws made in a block of clay. The kayakers were right — they had indeed been the victims of a hammerhead attack. I decided to dive down to the island's coral reef, and soon came across a stunning sight: dozens of scalloped hammerhead sharks swimming together in a school. These were mainly female sharks trying to catch the attention of the males, and they seemed uninterested in me. I suspected the attacks had happened when one or two hammerheads had mistaken the kayaks for prey swimming on the water's surface. To prevent any more attacks, I sent a bulletin across the island to warn swimmers, kayakers and surfers to stay out of the water at times when hammerheads hunt.

PERIGO
ÁREA SUJEITA
A ATAQUE
DE TUBARÃO

DANGER
RISK
OF SHARK ATTACK

THERE ARE NINE HAMMERHEAD SPECIES, EACH OF WHICH HAS A DIFFERENT VARIATION ON THE HAMMER-SHAPED HEAD.

SHARKS STATS

NAME: Scalloped hammerhead (*Sphyrna lewini*)

LENGTH: 1.5–4.3 metres

WEIGHT: Up to 155 kg

COLOUR: Greenish grey upper body with a white underside

RANGE: Temperate and tropical seas worldwide

LIFE SPAN: Up to 30 years

SENSING HEADS

With eyes at either end of its head, the hammerhead can see what is above it and below it at the same time. The hammerhead has super-sensitive electroreceptors and can track down stingrays buried under sand on the sea floor. The poisonous spines attached to a stingray's tail do not seem to affect hammerheads: I once observed one with over a hundred spines sticking out of its mouth. Hammerheads also eat a range of fish, as well as squid, octopus, lobster and other hammerheads!

ALTHOUGH THE HAMMERHEAD IS AN ACTIVE PREDATOR, IT IS NOT AMONG THE COMMON SHARK SPECIES THAT ATTACK HUMANS.

Sharks mate to produce baby sharks, called pups. Like mammals, most shark pups are born alive. But some shark species lay eggs protected by a leathery case known as a "mermaid's purse".

A NEWBORN BABY SHARK, BORN IN CAPTIVITY.

BIRTHING BABIES

Female sharks have the longest pregnancies of any animal on the planet. The spiny dogfish has a gestation period of up to 24 months. Sharks give birth to large litters. The blue shark, in particular, has been known to produce 100 pups. After it is born, the baby shark rests for a moment on the seabed, before swimming away and breaking the umbilical cord. Lots of shark pups do not survive long – adult sharks eat them. Many shark species are cannibals and eat members of their own families. Baby great whites, sand tigers, makos and thresher sharks even devour their own brothers and sisters while they are together in the womb.

A NEWBORN LEMON SHARK IS SHOWN STILL ATTACHED TO ITS MOTHER.

A SPINY DOGFISH WITH ITS
YOLK SAC STILL ATTACHED.
THIS GAVE THE SHARK
NOURISHMENT WHILE IN ITS
MOTHER'S WOMB.

LAYING EGGS

Sharks that lay their eggs include horn sharks, swell sharks, lesser spotted dogfish and bullhead sharks. Swell sharks protect their eggs by hiding them in seaweed. Long, string-like tendrils attached to the eggs curl around the seaweed to stop them being washed away. Horn sharks lay corkscrew-shaped eggs that they hide in gaps between rocks. A yolk sac inside in the case feeds the shark embryo as it develops.

THIS EGG CASE CONTAINING A
DEVELOPING BABY SHARK HAS
TENDRILS WHICH ATTACH AND
ANCHOR ONTO ROCKS.

Baby sharks can be savage. Once when I was examining the stomach contents of a dead sand tiger shark, I accidently put my hand into the shark's womb and was badly bitten by several unborn pups!

Seas and oceans cover 72 per cent of the world's surface. Yet, much remains unexplored by humans. As we are discovering the hidden corners of this underwater world, we are also finding new and unusual sharks. Often, these sharks are among the most weird and wonderful creatures ever seen on Earth.

MEGAMOUTH SHARK

The megamouth is a bizarre-looking deepwater shark that was first discovered in 1976 and has only been seen around 60 times since. Although it has up to 75 rows of small, hooked teeth, the megamouth is a filter-feeder. It sieves tiny plankton and soft-bodied creatures such as jellyfish from mouthfuls of water. During the day the megamouth descends to depths of around 300 metres, but at night it follows it prey upwards to around 12 metres.

ONE OF THE QUIRKS OF THE MYSTERIOUS MEGAMOUTH IS A MOUTH AT THE FRONT OF ITS HEAD, RATHER THAN THE UNDERSIDE.

COOKIECUTTER SHARK

The cookiecutter is a small, 48 centimetre-long shark which is a menace to large sea creatures. A bright, luminous colour, the cookiecutter attaches itself to animals such as seals, dolphins and whales with its cupped, sucker-like mouth. It then closes its jaws and twists its body around to cut out a "plug" of flesh, the size of a scoop of ice cream.

LONGNOSE SAW SHARK

The longnose saw shark has a snout, which is shaped like a chainsaw. Teeth on either side of the elongated snout are used to slash at prey and predators. The snout is also covered with electroreceptors and two, long barbells, which are used to detect food in the sea floor.

THE DWARF LANTERN SHARK IS ONE OF THE WORLD'S SMALLEST SHARKS, GROWING ONLY TO AROUND 20 CM LONG.

DWARF LANTERN SHARK

At 20 centimetres long, the dwarf lantern shark is the smallest shark in the world: and it also glows in the dark. It lives at depths of around 400 metres, and has light-emitting organs called photophores on its underside and fins. This phenomenon known as bioluminescence, helps the dwarf lantern shark stay camouflaged in sunlit waters and also attracts prey in the black waters of the deep.

THE FRILLED SHARK

The frilled shark lives near the bottom of the ocean and is only seen rarely. I came close to seeing a frilled shark alive. It had been caught by fishermen in Australia. I was nearby investigating a shark attack, but arrived too late to save the frilled shark. The fishermen were stunned by their catch, which looked like a sea monster, a prehistoric serpent from the deep.

The frilled shark is one of the oldest sharks in the world, alongside the goblin shark, and is believed to have been around for over 80 million years. It has an eel-like body, and eats by pushing out its jaws so they are wide enough to grab octopuses, squid, bony fish and other sharks. Scientists think it hunts by stealth: cruising through the water in search of prey and then making a sudden lunge, like a snake.

THE FRILLED SHARK IS HELPED IN ITS HUNT FOR FOOD BY ITS EXPOSED LATERAL LINE, SEEN HERE RUNNING ALONG THE SIDE OF ITS BODY.

SHARKS STATS

NAME: Frilled shark (*Chlamydoselachus anguineus*)
LENGTH: Up to 2 metres

COLOUR: Brown and grey
RANGE: The deep water of continental shelves and slopes
LIFE SPAN: Up to 50 years

THE FRILLED SHARK LIVES NEAR THE BOTTOM OF THE OCEAN AND IS SEEN VERY RARELY.

Sea Serpent Spooks Fishermen

A terrifying prehistoric shark which has 300 razor-sharp teeth has been caught by a fishing boat in Australia. The fisherman caught the shark in nets cast at about 1,000 metres deep and had no idea what the shark was. International shark expert Ben Hubbard, who happened to be investigating shark attacks in Western Australia at the time, was soon on the scene. Hubbard confirmed the shark to be the rare frilled shark, which is normally not seen out of the waters of the deep ocean.

"The frilled shark normally lives between 200 and 1,200 metres, which is the range fishermen are now casting their nets to catch the dwindling numbers of fish. It is a great shame for rare sharks such as this that they also have to die because of overfishing."

DEADLY KILLERS

A shark attack is a shocking sight. As the apex predators of the ocean, sharks are designed to hunt without fear or mercy. We often think of sharks as cold and heartless killers, but they have little interest in people. Humans have more chance of being struck by lightening than being eaten by a shark. And yet, dozens of attacks occur every year...

SHARK POSTURE

When a shark is about to attack it displays a "threat posture". This body language is easy to see if you are underwater: the shark raises its snout, arches its back and points its pectoral fins down. It may also curve its tail to one side or swim in a figure of eight.

THIS GREAT WHITE IS DISPLAYING ITS RELAXED, CRUISING POSTURE AND IS NOT AN IMMINENT THREAT.

KILLER COUNTDOWN

A shark attack often begins with blood in the water. A shark can smell blood from several hundred metres away and as it swims towards the scent, its other senses kick into action. First, a shark's ears and its lateral line system pick up the sounds and vibrations given off by the prey's movements. As it gets closer the shark's electroreceptors detect its victim's electrical signals, including its beating heart. When the shark spies its target, it accelerates to attack speed and takes a bite. Great whites and mako sharks often attack from below, and the power of their upward lunge can take them beyond the surface.

SEAL OR SURFER?

Attacks on surfers often take place near seal and sea lion colonies; the favourite prey of great white sharks. From underneath, surfers with their arms and legs dangling over the surfboard look a lot like seals. It has recently been discovered that much of a great white's brain is dedicated to its vision and helping the shark look upwards. This helps explain the number of great white attacks on surfers.

A SURFER SEEN FROM A SHARK'S PERSPECTIVE LOOKS DANGEROUSLY SIMILAR TO A SEAL.

SINGLE STRIKES

Nine out of 10 shark attacks on humans are single strikes. This is when a shark bumps, brushes past, or bites a person to find out if they're food. Shark injuries to people usually consist of cuts and abrasions, but sometimes whole limbs are lost. The victims of serious shark attacks often die from a loss of blood or are dragged under the waves and never seen again.

HUMANS OFTEN SEE GREAT WHITES AS MERCILESS MAN-EATERS, BUT THEY ARE FAR MORE INTERESTED IN DEVOURING SEALS THAN PEOPLE.

A SHARK ATTACK VICTIM SHOWING HIS HEALED SCARS.

Every year, between 70 and 100 shark attacks are reported worldwide. Around 12 of these attacks are fatal. But since many millions of people enter the ocean every year, this number is comparatively small. There is only a one in 11.5 million chance of being the victim of a shark attack. However, no-one's safety can be guaranteed in the water.

Surfing Shark Survivor

On Halloween morning, 2003, surfer Bethany Hamilton lost her left arm during an attack by a 4.5-metre tiger shark. Bethany was paddling on her surfboard in Kauai, Hawaii, when she felt: "a lot of pressure and a couple of lightning fast tugs. Then I watched in shock as the water around me turned bright red". After struggling to shore, Bethany was rushed to hospital. Despite losing 60 per cent of her blood, Bethany survived the attack and was back in the water three weeks later learning to surf with one arm. Today, Bethany wins professional surfing competitions around the world.

THE INDIANAPOLIS DISASTER

On July 28, 1945, American cruiser *USS Indianapolis* sailed through the waters of the Pacific Ocean after delivering parts for the atomic bomb that would later be dropped on Japan. Then, just after midnight, a torpedo from a Japanese submarine hit the *Indianapolis* and tore it in two. The ship sank in just 12 minutes, leaving 900 of the 1,196 men on board bobbing in the water. Soon afterwards, blue sharks and oceanic whitetips began feeding on the bodies of the dead. The men huddled together and tried to stay afloat, but the sharks began circling the survivors and picking off those with open wounds. The men who fought back and thrashed around in the water attracted more sharks, as did the cans of spam some of the sailors opened to eat. When rescuers finally arrived four days later only 300 men were left alive.

THE USS INDIANAPOLIS IN 1939, WHICH WAS TO SET THE STAGE FOR ONE OF THE GREATEST SHARK DISASTERS IN HISTORY.

ABOVE Bethany surfing in Hawaii.

THE JERSEY SHORE ATTACKS

The American Jersey Shore Attacks took place during an extreme heatwave in July, 1916. The first two shark attacks occurred within five days of each other: both were fatal. The same week, a boy was fatally bitten by a shark at the entrance of Matawan Creek and the man trying to save him was also killed. Only hours later, a shark grabbed a boy by his leg a few miles up the coast. The boy's father and brother managed to pull him free after a deadly tug of war with the shark. The attacks caused mass panic along the Jersey shore and rewards were offered to anyone who killed a shark. The attacks, which inspired the novel and movie *Jaws*, created a great hatred and fear of sharks which lasted for many decades. No-one is sure which species of shark was responsible for the attacks.

Shark Attack Teenager Died Saving Friend

The victim of the recent Barnacle Bay shark attack died while saving his best friend, it has been revealed. Sixteen-year-old kayaker James Morse tried to pull Ben Hubbard from the water after he had sustained a life-threatening bite to his leg. However, Hubbard's weight caused the kayak to capsize leaving Morse to be pulled under by the shark. His body has not been recovered. While Hubbard managed to escape to the shore he remains in a critical condition in Barnacle Bay hospital after a massive loss of blood. The shark responsible for the attacks, believed by experts to be a six-metre-long great white, is still at large.

My own tragic shark attack story occurred when I was 16. My best friend James and I were kayaking when we came across a group of dolphins huddled together and acting strangely. We decided to paddle away when something hit my kayak hard and knocked me into the water. I heard James yell "shark" as a huge dorsal fin raced toward me and I felt an explosion of pain on my left side. The next thing I remember is James whacking the shark with his paddle and hauling me onto his kayak. But his kayak overturned and then we were both in the water. I managed to grab hold of the kayak as a wave tossed me into the shallows. As I lay on the beach, I saw a large wound in my left thigh and an empty kayak beside me. James was gone.

I first came face to face with the fearsome tiger shark near the Island of Maui, Hawaii. Several shark attacks had been reported recently in the area and I was called in to find, tag and track some local tiger sharks. Tiger sharks are dangerous man-eaters with sharp, serrated teeth. I knew I would have to be careful.

ARMED WITH A DEADLY SENSE OF SMELL THAT CAN PICK UP BLOOD IN THE WATER FROM 400 METRES AWAY.

42

FOOD FOR THOUGHT

As I prepared my boat with shark tags and tracking devices, some fishermen showed me a dead tiger shark they found in their nets. We cut open the shark's stomach and were astonished with what we found: a half-eaten stingray, a seagull, a sea snake, a car licence plate and a woman's necklace. The last item filled me with horror: was this left over from an attack on a person?

ITEMS FOUND IN TIGER SHARK STOMACHS INCLUDE BOTTLES, LUMPS OF WOOD, CAR TIRES, A BAG OF COAL AND A SMALL DRUM.

COVERS DISTANCES OF 72 KILOMETRES EVERY 24 HOURS IN SEARCH FOR FOOD.

SHARKS STATS

NAME: Tiger shark (*Galeocerdo cuvier*)

LENGTH: 3–4.9 metres

WEIGHT: Up to 590 kg

COLOUR: Grey, green and blue with a pale underside. Has "tiger" stripes when young.

RANGE: Tropical and subtropical seas, from the shallows to depths of 300 metres

LIFE SPAN: 25 years plus

HIGHEST NUMBER OF ATTACKS ON HUMANS, ALONG WITH GREAT WHITES AND BULL SHARKS.

LOVE AT FIRST BITE

Tiger sharks can pose a serious threat to humans. A great white often stops attacking after the first bite, but a tiger shark will keep on eating! Within minutes of throwing fish bait into the water, a tiger shark appeared next to me and I quickly tagged its dorsal fin with my harpoon. I tagged nine more large tiger sharks during the night, which is their favourite time to hunt. Dark and murky waters allow tiger sharks to sneak up on their prey and then attack with bursts of speed that can reach 32 km/h.

FRIENDS

Sharks do not pose a risk to all creatures. Remoras, or shark-suckers, are 30-centimetre-long fish that swim alongside sharks or stick to them with special suckers on their heads. Remoras nibble off parasites from the sharks skin. Sharks also visit "cleaning stations" on coral reefs where they allow cleaner shrimps and wrasse to enter their mouths and gills and remove dead skin, scales, barnacles and tiny parasites.

FOOD

A shark usually eats once every two or three days and can survive for several weeks without eating by using up the food reserves stored in its liver. Meals vary from the tiny plankton eaten by whale sharks, to the large mammals consumed by predators such as the great white. A great white eats around 10 tonnes of meat every year to fuel its active lifestyle and help keep its blood warm.

REMORAS EITHER SUCK ONTO A SHARK OR SWIM ALONGSIDE IT, SNACKING ON THE REMAINS OF ITS MEALS.

A SEAL IS A HIGHLY NUTRITIOUS MEAL FOR A PURSUING SHARK.

FOES

Sharks have several enemies including larger sharks and hunting mammals, such as killer whales and sperm whales. Porpoises and dolphins will defend themselves by ramming their hard snouts into a shark's gills if under attack, and have been known to come to the aid of people in this way. But a more harmful enemy is much smaller: the parasite. Copepod parasites feed off a shark's eyeball causing blindness. Other parasites inhabit a shark's intestines, or live on its skin. Barnacles can attach themselves to a shark's fins, which irritate the shark and slow it down in the water. But the deadliest shark enemy of all is mankind.

THIS GREENLAND SHARK IS SHOWN WITH COPEPOD PARASITES, WHICH WILL EVENTUALLY MAKE IT BLIND.

Killer whales are highly intelligent and social animals that hunt in a pack, and are one of the few predators that pose a threat to a great white shark. When scientists play the recorded sounds of a killer whale underwater, sharks become highly agitated. Here, we see why: this great white stands no chance against the attacking pack of killer whales.

A shark feeding frenzy is a terrifying event. As a pack of sharks devours the food they spin, roll and thrash around and seem to bite at anything in their way. The tension mounts as a frenzy grows bigger and it only stops when all the food is gone.

GOING WILD

Normally a pelagic shark, such as the great white, cruises the ocean on autopilot looking for an opportunity to eat. When the shark detects prey, it instantly becomes alert and if it also picks up other sharks feeding, it will become agitated and follow the trail. From the outside, a feeding frenzy looks chaotic but it is controlled madness: the sharks are careful not to bite each other and concentrate only on the prey.

BLUE SHARKS FEED ON AN ANCHOVY "BAIT BALL" IN SOUTH AFRICA.

FLESH FEAST

A large carcass in the water, such as that of a whale, usually starts a feeding frenzy. As the first sharks find the carcass and start to tear off chunks, a response called a "supernormal stimulus" is sparked in nearby sharks. Frenzies have also been caused by large hauls of fish in a net and blood in the water.

A LARGE, ROTTING WHALE CARCASS IS PERFECT FODDER FOR A FEEDING FRENZY.

WHITETIP REEF SHARKS FEED EN-MASSE DURING THE NIGHT ON REEF FISH HIDING IN THE CORAL.

ABOVE Plesiosaurs were massive marine reptiles that lived 200–175 million years ago during the Jurassic period.

To: The Japanese Shark Association

From: Ben Hubbard

Dear Hideyoshi,

After examining the fossil of your prehistoric reptile, I can confirm that the creature died 85 million years ago during a shark feeding frenzy. Embedded in the reptile's skeleton were the remains of 80 shark teeth of different shapes and sizes – too many to belong to a single shark. The reptile, known as a plesiosaur, was around seven metres long, had powerful paddle-like arms and a mouth full of razor-sharp teeth. If it was still alive during the frenzy, it would have put up a good fight. But in the end it lost to the shark pack.

Yours sincerely,
Ben Hubbard

My first assignment as a shark biologist was to find and tag a bull shark. It was a terrifying prospect: bull sharks are aggressive and unpredictable man-eaters that can swim in fresh water. My mission was to travel up India's Ganges River and tag a rogue bull shark that had been harassing a village there. As I set out in my boat, I took a deep breath...

BULL SHARKS ARE KNOWN FOR THEIR STRENGTH AND UNPREDICTABILITY.

FRESHWATER TERROR

After I reached the small village on the banks of the Ganges River, the locals showed me the injuries of two boys who had been bitten by the bull shark. It was extraordinary that the shark had travelled hundreds of kilometres inland from the sea. Bull sharks use their unique freshwater tolerance to swim as far as 4,000 kilometres up river networks, where they hunt in warm, shallow and murky waters.

A BULL SHARK MOVES MENACINGLY THROUGH THE CALM WATERS OF A RIVER.

SAVAGE SHARKS

The bull shark gets its name from its short, blunt snout and its hunting method of head-butting a victim before biting. The bull shark typically consumes fish, dolphins and other sharks, although, like the tiger shark, it is not fussy about what it eats. The bull shark is a fierce and ferocious hunter but it can be attacked by bigger sharks, and at times, crocodiles.

SHARKS STATS

NAME: Bull shark, also known as the Zambezi shark (*Carcharhinus leucas*)

LENGTH: Up to 3.5 metres

WEIGHT: Up to 320 kg

COLOUR: Grey on top with a white underside

RANGE: The waters of the coasts of North and South America and Africa; along the Amazon, Mississippi and Ganges Rivers; and along the shores of South Asia and Australia. Favours shallow waters down to 31 metres.

After spending the night in the Indian village, I was awoken by a commotion by the river bank. I ran down to the water to see a massive crocodile battling with a bull shark. It was a fierce struggle, but the crocodile soon had the bull shark in its huge jaws. The predator that had bitten the boys from the village was no more.

Dying from a shark attack is rare: you have more chance of being killed by a snake, dog or wasp. But warming seas and declining numbers of fish are forcing sharks closer to shore. As the number of sharks and humans in the water have increased, so have the number of attacks. The following information will help you avoid an attack and also survive one!

CHAINMAIL JERKINS ARE A COMMON WAY OF PREVENTING LIFE-THREATENING SHARK BITES.

SHARK DETERRENTS

As I became famous as a shark expert, I was often asked to try out new shark deterrents for divers. A blue, camouflaged wetsuit which sharks find hard to see; and a black-and-white-striped wetsuit, which looks likes a poisonous sea snake have both fooled sharks. Devices that give off an electrical signal worn around the leg, arm or surfboard frighten sharks away. Special lights that flash in an approaching shark's face have also proved to be useful. To protect swimmers along the shoreline in shark-populated areas, underwater barriers are required. Shark nets made of rope and chainmail stop sharks coming too close. Another solution is a hose that releases a steady stream of bubbles upwards, which sharks won't swim through.

BE SHARK AWARE

Avoid swimming in murky water or at dawn, dusk or during the night, when sharks hunt. Always swim with friends, as sharks like to pick off lone victims. Never enter the water if you are bleeding and remove any jewellery that might sparkle like fish scales. Be aware of the marine life around you: seal colonies attract sharks, as do schools of "bait" fish in the water. These schools are easy to spot because they attract swooping seabirds.

WETSUITS WITH BLUE OR STRIPED PATTERNS ARE THOUGHT TO MAKE SWIMMERS LESS VISIBLE TO SHARKS.

SURVIVE AN ATTACK

Sharks are stealth hunters which launch surprise attacks quickly and without warning. You may not see a shark coming, but you can fight back if one attacks you. Punch and kick at an attacking shark's sensitive eyes and gills, or hit it with anything sharp or solid, like a camera. The main priority is to get back to shore. Swim as smoothly through the water as possible. Try not to panic or thrash around, as this will further excite the shark. Once on dry land seek out medical help – you'll need it at least for the shock if no worse injuries!

People are often surprised to learn that sharks are in serious trouble. Every year over 100 million sharks are caught by fishermen and their numbers are in decline. One quarter of all shark species are now in danger of becoming extinct. The top predator of the ocean could be wiped out by the top predator on Earth: people.

The best place to study sharks is in their natural ocean environment. But it can be hard to keep up with a shark! To see what sharks get up to when they swim out of view, scientists use the latest tagging and camera technology.

0433 XS

TELLING TAGS

Tags are the most common form of equipment used to monitor sharks. There are dozens of different kinds, which are usually attached to a shark's dorsal fin or placed beneath a shark's skin. The spikes and tags do not seem to bother the shark. Sometimes a tag is simply a plastic number but more sophisticated electronic tags send out signals that can be picked up via a receiving station or satellite. They also send alerts to shore patrols if a dangerous shark enters their waters. These tags provide scientists like me with valuable information about shark movements and behaviour.

MOST TAGS ARE INSERTED PAINLESSLY NEXT TO A SHARK'S DORSAL FIN.

CLEVER CAMERAS

New advances in camera technology let scientists observe sharks without having to risk their own safety. An underwater robotic device, known as an Automated Underwater Vehicle (AUV), picks up signals from a shark's tag and then tracks its movements. An AUV is fitted with several cameras. It can follow a shark for up to 130 kilometres before its batteries run low and it has to return to base. Scientists can also attach a mini camera to a shark's dorsal fin. The camera eventually falls off, floats to the surface, and sends off an electrical alert so it can be found. The footage from the camera then provides a shark's view of its underwater world.

SHARKCAM REMUS

PROPULSION SYSTEM

ANTENNA

REMUS GOPRO CAMERA

SHARK CAMERA MODULE

MAIN HOUSING

ELECTRONICS HOUSING

57

My love of sharks returned after I was able to handle lemon sharks in an aquarium. Lemon sharks are unusual because they do not seem to mind being touched by humans. They are calm, friendly and uninterested in attacking people. Being around lemon sharks is fascinating and fun. However, you still have to be careful of their sharp teeth!

A GREAT WHITE BITES DOWN ON A PIECE OF TAGGING APPARATUS.

WHALE SHARK

The whale shark is the largest fish in the ocean. It is longer than a bus, heavier than two elephants and has a massive, gaping mouth. Although it is the biggest of all sharks, the whale shark has a calm and gentle nature. After an eye-opening encounter with a school of whale sharks I made a promise to help protect them from people.

WHALE SHARKS ARE INSTANTLY-RECOGNIZABLE FROM THEIR METALLIC-BLUE BACKS COVERED WITH WHITE SPOTS.

MOUTHFULS OF FOOD

The whale shark has a wide, flat head and a 1.5-metre-wide mouth. Unlike the teeth of other sharks, a whale shark's teeth are the size of matchsticks and not used for feeding. The filter-feeding shark eats by straining mouthfuls of water through its gills. Tiny fish such as plankton are caught on special mesh filters and then swallowed whole. The whale shark does not have to swim forward to feed – it can lift itself into an upright position and then sink back down again to suck water and fish into its mouth.

MELLOW DRIFTERS

Whale sharks live in warm tropical waters where there is plenty of food and cruise near the surface at a slow three kilometres per hour. Boats have even been known to bump into the sharks and injure them with their propellers. Whale sharks are also in danger from fishermen, who hunt them for their meat, fins and liver oil. For this reason, whale sharks are endangered. But despite laws existing to protect them, hundreds of whale sharks are still caught every year.

SHARKS STATS

NAME: Whale shark (*Rhincodon typus*)

LENGTH: 5.5 to 12 metres

WEIGHT: Up to 21.5 tonnes

COLOUR: Grey, with pale yellow spots and stripes and a white belly

RANGE: Worldwide in tropical and temperate waters

LIFE SPAN: 20+ years

WHALE SHARKS HAVE HUNDREDS OF TINY TEETH WHICH ARE NOT USED FOR FEEDING.

WHALE SHARKS SCOOP UP PLANKTON IN THEIR COLOSSAL MOUTHS AS THEY SWIM CLOSE TO THE WATER'S SURFACE.

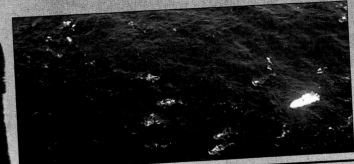

Scientist's Top Tag Tally

Shark Biologist Ben Hubbard was able to tag 15 whale sharks yesterday, as the largest ever gathering of the creatures continued off Mexico's Yucatan Coast. Hubbard said this raised his total number of tagged whale sharks to 29, as he continues his work to protect the endangered species from extinction.

In recent years, commercial fishing has turned the ocean's top predator into prey. The human appetite for shark meat and fins has had a devastating effect on shark numbers. It has been estimated that three sharks are killed every second. As the apex predator of the ocean, sharks keep the food chain in balance. Without sharks, the ocean environment would change for the worse.

RUBBISH AND POLLUTION ARE BOTH ADDING TO THE DEMISE OF MANY SHARK SPECIES.

FISHING TRAWLERS ACCIDENTALLY CATCH AND KILL MILLIONS OF SHARKS EVERY YEAR.

OVERFISHING

The fishing industry is the greatest threat to sharks. Many fishing boats use nets and long lines to target sharks such as hammerheads and dogfish for their meat, fins and liver oil. Other sharks are caught by accident in nets intended for fish. When this happens, the shark cannot move forwards to breathe and it usually suffocates. Often, their dead bodies are thrown away by the fishermen who have no use for them.

ANGLING

Hunting sharks is considered sport by anglers and shark jaws are often taken as trophies. Although only a few decades ago anglers were encouraged to hunt and kill sharks, today they are asked to release them back into the ocean.

POLLUTION

Climate change and dwindling numbers of fish worldwide are affecting shark movements. The warmer sea currents combined with the sharks' search for food are forcing them closer to land. Here, sharks pose a greater threat to people and they also find themselves in danger. Coastal waters often contain sewage, chemicals and rubbish. This waste is eaten by small fish, which in turn are eaten by bigger fish. Each time this happens the toxins become more concentrated, in a process called "bioamplification". Sharks are at the top of this food chain, so they absorb the highest doses of poison of all.

THIS HAMMERHEAD DROWNED BECAUSE IT WAS CAUGHT IN THE NET AND COULDN'T MOVE FORWARDS TO BREATHE.

MANY PEOPLE NOW UNDERSTAND THE IMPORTANCE OF PRESERVING OUR OCEANS AND THE CREATURES WHICH INHABIT THEM.

Dear Gill,

Thank you for your letter. I think the worst threat to sharks is "finning". This is when a fisherman cuts off a shark's fins and then throws it back into the sea. Without fins, the shark cannot swim and it drowns. The fins are then used in shark fin soup. If everybody in the world would stop eating this soup, then shark finning would end.

Yours sincerely,

Ben Hubbard

ACKNOWLEDGEMENTS

64

To the colleagues and friends who have braved the shark-infested depths with me: Rogo, Leti, Kim, Harv, Rach, FP, Nicko, Tom, Smit, Malc, Jody, and of course Monse, who would have been 42 this year. RIP.

The publishers would like to thank the following sources for their kind permission to reproduce the pictures in this book.

1. Brandon Cole/Naturepl.com, 2. (top left & centre) NHPA/Photoshot, (top right) Doc White/Naturepl.com, 3. Jeff Rotman/Naturepl.com, 4. Chris & Monique Fallows/Naturepl.com, 5. Author collection, 6-7. Chris & Monique Fallows/Naturepl.com, 8, 8-9, 9 (centre). Alex Mustard/Naturepl.com, 9. (bottom right) Ferdinand Lammot Belin Fund/National Gallery of Art, 10. (bottom) Ullstein Bild/Topfoto, 10. (centre) Jeff Rotman/Naturepl.com, 10-11. © Robert Nicholls/The Trustees of the Natural History Museum, London, 11. (bottom) Photoshot, (top) Ian Coleman/Naturepl.com, 12. (top left) Pascal Kobeh/Naturepl.com, (bottom left) Minden Pictures/Getty Images, 13. iStockphoto.com, 14. Michael Pitts/Naturepl.com, 14-15. Minden Picture/Getty Pictures, 15. (top right) Ocean's Image/Photoshot, 18. Chris & Monique Fallows/Naturepl.com, 18-19. & 19. NHPA/Photoshot, 20-21. Imagebroker/Photoshot, 22. (left) Alex Hyde/Naturepl.com, 22. (centre) Juan Manuel Borrero, 22-23. Pascal Kobeh/Naturepl.com, 23. (left) Oceans Image/Photoshot, (centre) Brandon Cole/Naturepl.com, (right) Alex Mustard/Naturepl.com, (bottom), Jeff Rottman/Naturepl.com, 24. (bottom left) NHPA/Photoshot, (centre) VWPics/Photoshot, 24-25. NHPA/Photoshot, 25. Jeff Rotman/Naturepl.com, 26-27 Mint Images/Photoshot, 28. (bottom left) Brandon Cole/Naturepl.com, (bottom) Photoshot, 28-29 Wildestanimal/Getty Images, 29. (right) Jim Abernethy/Barcroft Media/Getty Images, (bottom) Shutterstock.com, 30. (top) Justin Sullivan/Getty Images, (bottom) Doug Perrine, 30-31. Photoshot, 31. (centre) DeAgostini/Getty Images, 32. (bottom) AFP Photo/Toru Yamanaka/Getty Images, 32-33 Bruce Rasner/Rotman/Naturepl.com, 33. (top) Roberto Nistri/Alamy Stock Photo, (centre) Stephen Frink Collection/Alamy Stock Photo, (bottom) Javontae Murph, 34 (bottom) & 34-35. NHPA/Photoshot, 35. Andia/Photoshot, 36-37. Bruce Coleman/Photoshot, 38. (left) Mark Carwardine/Naturepl.com, (bottom) Chris & Monique Fallows/Naturepl.com, 38-39. Doug Perrine/Naturepl.com, 39. (top) David Fleetham/Naturepl.com, (bottom) Jeff Rotman/Naturepl.com, 40. (centre) National Archives and Records Administration, Washington, 40-41. David Gregerson/Sport Studio Photos/Getty Images, 41. (top right) Private Collection, 42-43. David Doubilet/National Geographic Creative/Corbis, 43. (bottom) Jurgen Freud/Naturepl.com, 44-45. NHPA/Photoshot, 45. (top) Franco Banfi/Naturepl.com, (bottom) NHPA/Photoshot, 46-47. (top) Brandon Cole/Naturepl.com, (bottom) Oceans Image/Photoshot, 48. (bottom left) Chris & Monique Fallows/Naturepl.com, 48-49. Brandon Cole/Naturepl.com, 49. (top) NHPA/Photoshot, (bottom) © The Trustees of the Natural History Museum, London, 50. NHPA/Photoshot, 50-51. Gerard Soury, 51. Andrew Paice/Getty Images, 52. Bruce Coleman/Photoshot, 52-53. SMS/Splash News/Corbis, 54-55. Richard Herrmann, Visuals Unlimited/Science Photo Library, 56. Roger Munns, Subazoo/Science Photo Library, 56-57. Oceans Image/Photoshot, 57. Vimeo/Woods Hole Oceanographic Institute, 58-59. (main shark) Wildestanimal/Getty Images, (cage) Oceans Image/Photoshot, 60. Brandon Cole/Naturepl.com, 60-61. Steve De Neef/VWPics, 61. Oscar Reyes, 62. Philip Stephen/Naturepl.com, 62-63. Jeff Rotman/Naturepl.com, 63. (top) Imagebroker.net/Photoshot, (bottom) Lou Dematteis/Spectral Q via Getty Images, 64. Look/Photoshot

All other images Freeimages.com, iStockphoto.com & Shutterstock.com

Every effort has been made to acknowledge correctly and contact the source and/or copyright holder of each picture and Carlton Books Limited apologises for any unintentional errors or omissions that will be corrected in future editions of this book.